"I'm so happy that Elisa Nebolsine wrote this book ⟨ topic of grit! Elisa is an exceptional psychotherapist, understanding of cognitive behavioral therapy (CBT, user-friendly for children. This book teaches kids about the skills that contribute to perseverance and resilience, including mindfulness, stress management, and CBT skills for self-assessment, problem-solving, and talking back to self-defeating thoughts. Elisa encourages kids to engage in a number of exercises for developing these skills and putting them into action—and she offers them tools for charting their progress in each area. *The Grit Workbook for Kids* is written in a conversational style that is clear, straightforward, and encouraging, but does not talk down to kids. And the wonderful illustrations help to make the book accessible to children. It's a winning combination that makes this an important new contribution to the library of self-help books for young people."

> —**Bill Stixrud, PhD**, clinical neuropsychologist, and coauthor of
> *The Self-Driven Child*

"*The Grit Workbook for Kids* is a great resource for children who struggle with anxiety, self-doubt, isolation, depression, or low self-esteem. The concept of identifying, practicing, and growing grit is genius! This practical, engaging book has tons of great ideas and lessons. Nebolsine has great confidence that children are capable of positive change because she has a stellar and successful career helping children using a playful, cognitive-behavioral approach. I'm grateful that she's sharing her innovative concepts and strategies."

> —**Eliana Gil, PhD**, founder, partner, and senior clinical and research
> consultant at the Gil Institute for Trauma Recovery and Education in
> Fairfax, VA

"This workbook is an invaluable resource for anyone with children in their lives—parents, teachers, child care providers, and others. It is a very clear and understandable guide to teaching kids skills that will empower them to succeed in all areas of their lives—be it socially, academically, or on the sports field. The wealth of information it provides is not to be missed!"

> —**Beth Salcedo, MD, DFAPA**, past president of the Anxiety and Depression
> Association of America, and medical director at The Ross Center

"*The Grit Workbook for Kids* offers practical, important, and evidence-based strategies for kids to improve their perseverance, perspective, and problem-solving skills. The explanations are clear, the illustrations engaging, and the activities substantial. Every child can benefit from building his or her GRIT!"

—**Mary K. Alvord, PhD**, psychologist, and coauthor *Conquer Negative Thinking for Teens* and *Resilience Builder Program for Children and Adolescents*

"Elisa Nebolsine has done a masterful job with *The Grit Workbook for Kids*. It is accessible and helpful to children and parents alike. She explains complex concepts such as growth mindset and resiliency in simple and practical terms. The basics of affective brain science are presented in a nontechnical and understandable manner. Each new idea is accompanied with an exercise that puts it into action, building a new skill. Skills build on other skills, developing a range of tools and techniques for preserving and succeeding in the face of the routine stresses and strains in a child's daily life. This is an outstanding addition to the self-help literature for children."

—**Gary R. VandenBos, PhD**, senior professional consultant for the National Register of Health Service Psychologists, and coauthor of *Leaving It at the Office*

"*The Grit Workbook for Kids* is outstanding! It is a very helpful book for children and their parents. It is well written, engaging, interesting, fun for the reader, and chock-full of helpful information and practical coping techniques. The artwork and graphics enhance the book, helping the exercises and text come alive. This workbook focuses on building grit, resilience skills, and a growth mindset. But these exercises also teach children skills to manage their everyday challenges and stresses. Professionals who work with children, regardless of their specific approach, will find this book an asset. I am eager to use it with children in my practice, and recommend it to parents to broaden their children's ability to persevere and bounce back when life becomes challenging. This is a winner!"

—**Jane Annunziata, PsyD**, clinical psychologist in McLean, VA; and coauthor of *Shy Spaghetti and Excited Eggs* and seven other psychological books for children

The Grit Workbook for Kids

CBT Skills to Help Kids Cultivate a Growth Mindset & Build Resilience

ELISA NEBOLSINE, LCSW

Instant Help Books
An Imprint of New Harbinger Publications, Inc.

Publisher's Note

Distributed in Canada by Raincoast Books

Copyright © 2020 by Elisa Nebolsine
      Instant Help Books
      An imprint of New Harbinger Publications, Inc.
      5674 Shattuck Avenue
      Oakland, CA 94609 www.newharbinger.com

Cover design by Amy Shoup; Cover photo is a model and for illustrative purposes only. Acquired by Jess O'Brien; Edited by Karen Schader

---

Library of Congress Cataloging-in-Publication Data

Names: Nebolsine, Elisa, author.
Title: The grit workbook for kids : CBT skills to help kids cultivate a growth mindset and build resilience / Elisa Nebolsine.
Description: Oakland, CA : New Harbinger Publications, [2020]
Identifiers: LCCN 2020019881 (print) | LCCN 2020019882 (ebook) | ISBN 9781684035984 (trade paperback) | ISBN 9781684035991 (pdf) | ISBN 9781684036004 (epub)
Subjects: LCSH: Resilience (Personality trait) in children--Juvenile literature. | Mindfulness (Psychology)--Juvenile literature. | Cognitive therapy for children--Juvenile literature.
Classification: LCC BF723.R46 N43 2020 (print) | LCC BF723.R46 (ebook) | DDC 155.4/191--dc23
LC record available at https://lccn.loc.gov/2020019881
LC ebook record available at https://lccn.loc.gov/2020019882

Printed in the United States of America

22 21 20

10 9 8 7 6 5 4 3 2 1   First Printing

For Ellie, Riley, Kiki, and Nick. You are my favorites.

Contents

Foreword

Kids today face a barrage of challenges, and rates of anxiety and depression are on the rise. Whether at school, at home, on the playground, or during activities, an extra degree of grit can help them overcome the challenges they face every day. And as Elisa Nebolsine shows in this excellent workbook, kids can not only use grit to deal with what life throws them, but they can also learn to build up their grit and their resilience. The workbook starts by empowering kids and showing them that they can learn to build the skills of grit. It then moves into strategies for "growing grit" and concludes with practical and effective techniques for kids to use in the real world. It's an excellent resource!

The workbook draws from the evidence-based principles of cognitive behavioral therapy (CBT). CBT is considered the gold standard for psychological help for adults and for children. When my father, Aaron T. Beck, MD, developed CBT (back in the 1970s), he did so with the idea that clients should learn and practice skills. CBT was adapted decades ago for children, and the research supporting the efficacy of CBT with kids is long-standing, far-reaching, and significant.

When I first started my professional life, I taught children with learning disabilities. Many of them lacked grit. I wish I had had this workbook to use with them then. CBT and grit are a natural fit. The core idea of CBT is that it is not a situation but our *perception* of a situation that leads us to have negative reactions. If we're under stress, our perceptions (that is, the thoughts that pop into our minds) are often inaccurate and/or unhelpful. When we change these thoughts, we can change how we feel and, just as importantly, how we act. Grit requires tenacity and perseverance, and those tendencies are not always natural responses to a situation. It takes effort to change our responses, to not quit prematurely, and to learn to keep going, even when the going is tough. CBT provides the skill set for these changes, and this workbook applies these critical concepts to kids.

The Grit Workbook for Kids is an important resource for parents, caregivers, teachers, therapists, medical providers—and anyone else who interacts with kids. It's clear, understandable, and fun. The book teaches kids the skills they need to build their grit, and the engaging exercises let kids learn and generalize these skills.

I encourage you to read and use this workbook with the children in your life. Teaching kids these skills at a young age can provide them with the extra grit that will better equip them to handle the unexpected and the growing challenges of modern life. And, I predict, this toolbox of creative ideas and strategies may also be personally helpful to you.

—Judith S. Beck, PhD
President, Beck Institute for Cognitive Behavior Therapy
Clinical Professor of Psychology in Psychiatry, University of Pennsylvania

Letter for Parents

Does your child give up a little too soon when things get tough? Melt down easily? Get stuck in certain ways of thinking or reacting? If so, this book is for you.

It's not easy to be a kid! Increasing demands on children—longer hours spent on schoolwork, more scheduled activities, and less free time to play and relax—are creating greater stresses and challenges for young people. Kids face a lot of pressure to do well in school and prepare themselves for future success.

You already know intuitively that persistence makes a difference in life. Now research is bearing that out. Studies by Angela Duckworth, an internationally regarded psychologist, university professor, and researcher, as well as others have shown that success is not a matter of IQ or talent; what sets high achievers apart is *grit*, or the ability to persist in difficult situations. Developing grit helps both adults and children become more successful across many domains in life. When adults practice grit they achieve more, and they also model persistence and resiliency for their children.

Grit is what enables kids to persevere in working toward their goals even when the going gets tough. It's how they tolerate discomfort and achieve the rewards of accomplishments that require effort. Grit is key to kids doing the hard things they want or need to do, whether that's getting good grades, making a travel team, or building an awesome treehouse.

As parents, we often wish to make things easier for our children. No one wants to see their child suffer. Yet, it's impossible to protect children from discomfort. In fact, if we try to make life too comfortable for kids so they never experience adversity, we actually put them at a disadvantage. The ability to deal positively with obstacles and disappointments is crucial for good mental health.

Fortunately, you don't have to be born "gritty." Grit is something children (and adults) can learn. It's possible for kids to develop new skills to enable them to bounce back from tough situations and see obstacles differently. *The Grit Workbook for Kids* offers twenty-eight fun, engaging activities that help kids learn and practice the tools, strategies, and skills that make up grit. These activities cover:

- *Building stamina* (taking care of your body and mind by improving sleep, eating, exercise, and relaxation)

- *Keeping perspective* (seeing a situation accurately; noticing the good options and possibilities)

- *Being optimistic* (choosing to stay hopeful even when things aren't going your way; training your brain to look for the positive)

- *Solving problems* (identifying the issue, brainstorming possible solutions, choosing one, and trying it out)

- *Coping with change* (dealing with the unknown and uncertainty; bouncing back from unexpected challenges)

- *Practicing flexibility* (being open to new experiences and different ideas)

- *Sticking up for yourself* (advocating for what you need or want)

- *Building good relationships* (making connections with people who can support you and help you)

- … and much more.

Your child can use this book independently or you can use it together. As needed, please help your child access the content that is available online at http://www .newharbinger.com/45984.

While the activities do build on each other, I've designed them so that you can go back to earlier topics for a refresher or skip straight to the ones you need.

Grit is not about avoiding every pothole in the road of life. It's about gaining traction and moving ahead without getting stuck. Childhood is the ideal time to learn grit, because the earlier skills are taught, the more easily they become natural responses. *The Grit Workbook for Kids* gives kids—and the adults who care about them—a wealth of valuable tools for building this essential life skill.

Introduction for Kids

Have you ever felt like something was just too hard for you to do? You see other kids doing it, and it looks easy for them, but when you try, it seems to take forever or fall apart. Do you ever feel like giving up even though you know you should keep going? Does it ever seem like everyone else has it easier than you, and you don't know why it feels that way?

If so, this book is for you. It was written for kids who want to be able to stick with things longer and to feel more confident about what they can do. It's for kids who know they can do hard things but sometimes have a hard time figuring out how to keep going. It's for kids who have ideas about things they want or need to do, but don't know how to get them over the finish line. In short, it's for kids who want to build their grit.

This book is designed to be a tool for you to learn the skills needed to become grittier. The book works best if you start at the beginning and follow it in order, because the skills it teaches build on each other. It's kind of like learning an instrument. First you learn how to hold the instrument, how to make it create sounds, then you learn how to make different notes. Finally, you combine the notes to make music. That's how this book works; all the different steps come together to teach you the skills of grit.

That doesn't mean you have to go at the same pace on every page. As you work your way through the book, you may notice you are already pretty strong in some areas. You may also notice some areas that are really challenging for you. If so, you can decide that you don't need to spend as long on the areas you already know well. Hopefully, you will also decide to put in extra effort on the areas where you need to grow.

Grit grows best with regular practice. The skills you learn from this workbook will need to be put into action in your everyday life. The more you practice and learn from them, the bigger you will build your grit. This won't be an easy process, but you can do it. And it will be worth the effort. When you are gritty, you stick with things that are hard without easily giving up. You focus on what you can do, and feel strong in yourself rather than comparing yourself to others and wishing you were like them. Building grit makes you feel good about yourself and your abilities.

Some of the activities include online material you can download. Ask your parents to help you register for and access that material. It's also okay to ask for help if you're struggling with parts of the book. Your parents may be able to help you, or you may even be able to ask a teacher or guidance counselor. Asking for help is actually an important part of building grit.

At the end of this book, will you be able to climb mountains and scale buildings? Probably not. But that's not what grit is really about. By the end of this book, you will know the skills and strategies needed to be your grittiest self. Everyone's grittiest self looks different, but maybe yours will be able to get through difficult homework that used to knock you down. Maybe yours will stick with learning a new sport you really wanted to learn but felt was too hard for you. Or maybe you will try something new rather than assuming it won't work out. That's even better than scaling a building.

As you read through remember: the more you work at this, the bigger your grit will grow.

You got this!

Ryan wanted to try out for the school play, and he wanted to get the lead role. He spent a lot of time practicing his part, and he knew all the lines. Guess what? Ryan didn't get the part he wanted. He was given the part of a villager instead. His villager had only three lines. Ryan was so disappointed.

Instead of giving up or quitting, he decided to become the best villager in the play. He worked on his costume, and he practiced his lines in front of the mirror every day. He experimented with different ways of speaking them—louder or softer, funny, or more serious—and he tried different ways of moving his arms and body. Ryan's teacher noticed that he was improving his acting skills. When the play was over, she encouraged him to check out a nearby children's theater. Ryan is now taking acting classes, and he is slowly getting more time on stage. Ryan showed grit. He kept going even when he was disappointed.

For You to Know

Grit sounds like a funny word, but grit is actually an important trait that you can learn. When kids show grit, it means they stick with something that is hard and they keep going … even when they want to give up. A researcher named Angela Duckworth has studied grit for years, and she has learned that kids who show grit tend to stick with things longer and feel better about their efforts. Dr. Duckworth has shown that you don't have to be naturally talented at something to get better at it.

Some of us seem to be born with more grit than others, but that doesn't matter. Even if you aren't naturally supergritty, you can build your grit. Grit is a skill you can learn, just like learning to dribble a basketball, draw a horse, or write in cursive. The more you learn about grit, and the more you practice it, the grittier you'll become. You really can get better at sticking with things and not giving up. You'll feel strong and proud when you know you can push through tough situations and keep going.

Ryan is a great example of grit—and so are you. You are already practicing grit! Think back to a time or two when you wanted to give up but kept going.

Have you ever

- taken a hard test and still made sure to check your answers before turning it in?

- run the mile at school when you really didn't want to?

- gone to a party even though you were nervous?

- tried out for a team or a play even though it was scary?

When you did those things, you were showing grit. It may not seem like a big deal, but it is. Sticking with things you don't want to do or don't think you can do well is not easy. But every time you keep going and don't quit, you are helping your grit grow bigger and stronger.

For You to Do

Read these stories, and circle examples of kids who are practicing grit.

Caitlyn has just learned how to skateboard. She isn't very good at it yet, but she's getting better every time she practices. She's careful about where she skates, and she always wears her helmet and pads. One day she hits a bump, loses her balance, and falls to the ground. Her leg is scratched, but it's not too bad. And even though she may end up with a bruise, the pads and helmet kept her mostly safe. Her mom runs over and asks if she's okay. Caitlyn says, "I think so. My leg hurts, but it's really not that bad. Is it okay if I keep practicing?"

Morgan is on a new soccer team, and the coach is mean. He yells at everyone, and Morgan starts to dread practice each day. She tells her dad that she wants to quit the team. Her dad asks her to think about it for a day or two before deciding. Morgan thinks it over, and then asks her dad if he will go with her to talk to the coach. Morgan loves soccer, but she doesn't like the way the coach yells at people. Morgan's dad agrees, and they go talk to the coach together.

Matt has to take a big test at school. He knows it's important, and he's very worried. What if he doesn't know the answers? What if he fails? Matt reads the first question, and he gets even more worried. He doesn't know what to write. The same thing happens on the second question. He can feel his heart pounding. He's sure he is going to fail. He really wants to just guess the answers and get it over with. Why bother trying when he's only going to fail? Instead, Matt takes a deep breath and decides to do his best. He writes the best answer he can for each question.

Did you circle all three? If so, good for you. These kids are all showing grit. Sometimes grit is big and obvious, and sometimes it's small and hard to spot. In every case, though, these kids found a way to stick with something they wanted or needed to do.

As you learn more about grit, you will get better and better at noticing it in yourself and others.

How Gritty Are You?

Suzy was mad! She had lost her soccer game, she couldn't find her shin guards, and she was tired and hot. Her parents reminded her that she had to hurry to the car so they could get home and get ready for a birthday dinner for her aunt. Suzy lost it. She started to yell and then to cry. At that moment she wasn't feeling very gritty. In fact, Suzy struggles with grit a lot of the time. She finds it very hard not to give up or to give in to big feelings.

For You to Know

Some of us naturally have more grit, and some of us naturally have less. That's okay. We can build grit in our brains the same way we can build muscles in our bodies. What do you do if you want to make your muscles stronger? Maybe you do push-ups to strengthen your arms. Or maybe you decide to start jumping rope so you can have more strength in your legs. Building grit is done exactly the same way: with practice and effort.

For You to Do

To get a better sense of your current grit level, complete this chart. For each statement on the left, mark the column that best describes you. For example, if you never enjoy a challenge, you'd put a 0 in the column headed *Not true at all*. If you get super-excited at every challenge, you'd put a 3 in the column headed *Very true.*

Total your score at the bottom of each column, and add those four totals to get your grand total.

	Not true at all (0)	*A little true* (1)	*True* (2)	*Very true* (3)
I love a challenge!		X		
I have a hard time finishing projects I start.		X		
I enjoy completing difficult tasks.	X			
If I fail at something, I want to give up or quit.			X	
My parents and teachers say I work very hard.	X	X		
Practicing isn't worth it. I don't think it helps.		X		
Total	/	3	2	/
Grand total	5	3	2	

Take a look at your answers. If your grand total is 16 or higher, you already have a high grit level, but that doesn't mean you can't get grittier. This book can help you build your grit even more!

If your grand total is 15 or below, your answers show that grit can be a little harder for you, and that's okay. Get ready to grow your grit as you work through this book.

No matter what you scored, we're so glad you're reading this book!

Tracking Your Grit Level

Jackson was having a hard week. On Monday he got in big trouble for stomping out of the classroom because he didn't understand how to do the math problems. On Tuesday he got in trouble at home because he wouldn't do his math homework, and he told his mom it was just too hard for him to try. But on Wednesday he decided he needed to learn how to do this math. He met with his teacher before school and again at lunch to get extra help. He worked and worked until he understood it.

For You to Know

No one's grit level is always at a 10. Jackson did not show much grit at the beginning of the week, but on Wednesday he was supergritty. Our grit levels go up and down just like the temperature outside. We can't predict our grit levels as accurately as a weather forecaster can predict the temperature, but we can learn more about when it's easy for us to be gritty and when it's harder.

The picture below is a grit thermometer. You can use it as a tool to measure your grit levels. Tracking your grit levels lets you know when you are most able to be gritty, and when you have to work harder for grit. The more you pay attention to your grit levels, the more you learn about the areas you need to build.

10. I will finish!
9. I got this!
8. I will figure out a way to do this!
7. I will try!
6. I can't do this yet, but I will do it soon.
5. I'm not sure I want to do this.
4. This is getting hard.
3. This is hard!
2. No way!
1. I am NOT doing this!

For You to Do

Let's give the grit thermometer a try. Here's how it works. If Jackson rated his grit level on Monday when he stormed out of the classroom, it would be a 1: "I am *not* doing this!" On Tuesday when he refused to do his homework, his rating might be a 2: "No way!" But on Wednesday, when he asked for extra help and pushed himself to work until he understood the math, his grit level was a 10: "I will finish!" Over the course of three days, Jackson's grit level changed quite a bit.

Think back to a time this week when you showed grit. Maybe you were able to do thirty sit-ups in PE class or maybe you finished every single vocabulary word in your homework. Using the thermometer, choose the number that best corresponds to your grit level that day.

Grit rating: _____

Now remember a time this week when you found it very hard to keep going. This might have been when you got a lower grade than you expected on a test. Or maybe it was when you were the first one out in a game at recess. No shame! We all have things that are harder for us to do and things that are easier. Think of a time this week when you didn't show as much grit. Now rate that moment on the thermometer.

Grit rating: _____

Now that you've got the hang of using the grit thermometer, let's try to use it for a full week.

To track your grit, write down:

- what was going on at the time;

- your grit temperature rating;

- the thoughts that were going through your head at the time.

The form below lets you track this information. You can download the thermometer and tracking form at http://www.newharbinger.com/45984. And if you want someone to help, that's fine!

DAY & TIME	SITUATION (DESCRIBE WHAT HAPPENED)	GRIT TEMPERATURE RATING	WHAT I WAS THINKING TO MYSELF
Sunday around dinnertime	I needed to finish my homework, and I didn't want to do it. I made myself sit down and do it.	8	"You can do this. Just get it over with."

The Grittiest of Them All

Jake was the shortest kid in his class. He was actually the shortest kid in both classes on his grade level. A lot of people assumed that Jake wasn't much of an athlete because of his size. But Jake's size had nothing to do with his grit level.

Jake played soccer, and the other kids on the team were bigger and stronger than he was. Jake knew he couldn't change his height, but he decided to become the fastest runner and best ball handler on the team. He practiced every day, and he focused on improving his weakest areas. His hard work paid off, and he was a sought-after striker in school and on his team. Jake was small, but he was gritty!

For You to Know

You've probably heard the expression "you can't judge a book by its cover," so you already know that how someone looks on the outside doesn't always show how gritty they are on the inside. Some people have huge muscles that make them look strong, but that doesn't mean they won't give up when things get tough. Some people seem shy or quiet, but they stick with things others would avoid. Grit is about how people choose to think and act, not about how they look.

CBT Skills to Help Kids Cultivate a Growth Mindset & Build Resilience

For You to Do

Do you remember in *Snow White* when the witch looks in the mirror and asks, "Who is the fairest of them all?" If you were to ask the magic mirror who is the grittiest person of them all, what do you think it would tell you? Who is the grittiest person you can think of? It might not be someone you know personally, and that's okay. Just make sure the person or people you choose are gritty on the inside where it counts the most!

Write the name of the grittiest person you can think of inside the mirror on the next page. Under their name, write a few words or draw something that describes what makes that person gritty on the inside. Remember, grit does not necessarily look like big muscles on the outside!

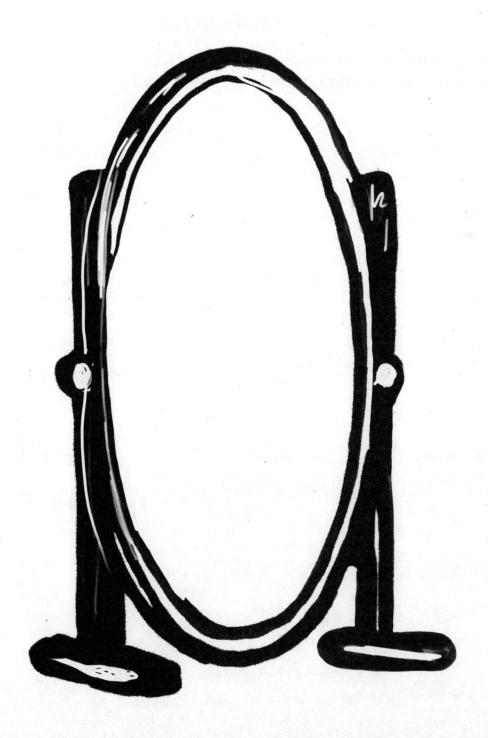

More to Do

What would feel different about you if you were supergritty? Circle the feelings you would feel if you were supergritty.

brave	excited	happy
strong	scared	satisfied
determined	confident	uncertain
hopeful	nervous	worried
enthusiastic	proud	joyful

On separate pieces of paper, write the words you chose, and write them with feeling! If you chose "strong," you might add some muscles to the letters. If you chose "happy," you might add rays of sunlight beaming out from the word. Here's an example using the word "brave":

Grit Spotting

Lily loved the color pink. She had pink shoes, pink clothes, pink everything. She noticed there were no pink cars on the roads, and she was so disappointed. How could there be a world without pink cars? But then, she started to keep an eye out for pink cars, and bam! *she started seeing them everywhere. She just had to really* look *for them.*

For You to Know

The same is true with grit. Grit can show up in ways both big and small, which means that sometimes it's easy to see and sometimes we have to look hard to find it. But once we start looking for grit, we start noticing it more and more, and eventually we see it everywhere. Even better, noticing the grit around you actually helps you build your own supply. The more you see it, the more possible it becomes. We'll call this skill grit spotting.

Grit spotting is actually fun. You might notice grit in the squirrel who wouldn't give up until it got the birdseed out of the feeder, or you might see it in your little sister when she is determined to learn to ride her bicycle. Grit is all around us, and once you start looking, you're going to see it all over the place!

For You to Do

Ready, set, go—start looking! To fill in your grit-spotting finds, use the form below or download a copy at http://www.newharbinger.com/45984. You can draw or write yourself, or ask someone for help.

· GRIT SPOTTING ·

**SPOTTED AT SCHOOL.
I SAW MY CLASSMATE
SHOW GRIT WHEN**

_____
_____
_____
_____

**MY FAMILY HAS GRIT.
I SAW IT WHEN**

_____
_____
_____
_____

**GRIT IN NATURE.
I SAW IT WHEN**

_____
_____
_____
_____

**GRIT IN ME!
I SHOWED IT WHEN**

_____
_____
_____
_____

Brains Can Change

For You to Know

Squeaker is a rat. He lives in a cage full of puzzles, books, and things to climb. Every day he is very busy trying new activities and solving puzzles.

Shaggy is also a rat. He lives in a plain cage. He doesn't do much, other than play video games. If he had YouTube, he would just lie on a rat sofa and watch all day long.

Ready for an amazing fact? Squeaker's brain weighs more than Shaggy's. Squeaker's brain has more nerve connections that make it heavier than Shaggy's. Squeaker made those connections himself through all his activity. Squeaker actually made himself smarter by using his brain so much in ways that challenge him physically and mentally.

Rats aren't the only animals that can get smarter. Humans can also get smarter. Intelligence can actually grow. In the past, people thought our intelligence was set, like our height or the color of our eyes, and that we couldn't get any smarter. But scientists have found that's not true, and that we can actually get smarter by doing things that challenge our brains.

Like muscles, our brains get stronger with practice, challenge, and repetition. The more we push ourselves to learn hard information, and the more we stick with it, the more our brains learn.

For You to Do

Write "yes" or "no" on the line before each of these questions:

_____   Think of a student at your school or a friend who is really good at skateboarding. Imagine that person. Do you see that friend with their skateboard a lot?

_____   Think of a student at your school or a friend who is an excellent musician. Get a picture of that person in your mind. Does that person practice a lot?

_____   Think of a student at your school or a friend who is really good at gymnastics. Picture that person. Do they seem to be doing cartwheels all the time?

_____   Think of a student at your school or a friend who is a great reader. Visualize that person. If you found them right now, would they have a book in their hand?

_____   Think of a student at your school or a friend who is really good at solving the Rubik's Cube. When you imagine that person, are they holding the cube?

Did you write "yes" for most of the answers? If so, you know there is a connection between practice, learning, and skill. Shaggy is not going to win any skateboarding competitions if he's always on the couch. In order to get better at something, to make our brains stronger and heavier, we have to practice.

The Grit Workbook for Kids

For You to Know

Squeaker and Shaggy both have brains that are capable of learning and making more connections. So do you! Ready to learn even more about how your brain works?

Is your brain about the size of a guinea pig, a hamster, or a cat? If you guessed guinea pig, then you're right! Your brain weighs about three and a half pounds. Unfortunately, your brain is not quite as cute as a guinea pig....

Have you ever seen a picture of a real brain? Our brains are grayish and lumpy. They aren't very pretty, but they are pretty cool! Two parts of the brain that matter for building grit are called the *amygdala* (ah-MIG-da-la) and the *prefrontal cortex*, or the PFC. Those words sound big and fancy, but we can understand them better if we look at them as if they were animals.

Let's start with the amygdala. See the dog below? We'll call her Amygdala Annie. Annie's a nice dog who only wants the very best for you, and who always tries to keep you safe. Unfortunately, in her eagerness to perform her job, Annie sometimes barks way too much and overreacts for silly reasons.

Amygdala Annie has a hard time seeing the difference between a real danger (angry bear!) and a temporary stress (big test!). When Annie starts barking, she goes into full-on protection mode, and she doesn't think, she just reacts. This is good for getting you to run away when you see an angry bear, but it's not so good when you can't think during a test.

PFC Pete is the other part of the brain we are going to learn about. Pete is a wise owl, and he is great at solving problems, making decisions, and giving advice.

Pete is the one you need when you're taking a test, learning a new skill, or doing anything that requires deep thinking. Pete is wise and organized, and he's great at being in charge. When we are calm and in control, it means PFC Pete is running the show.

We *want* Pete to be in charge. He manages our homework and helps us remember what we studied; he helps us treat others respectfully; he helps us stay organized;

he helps us make all kinds of better decisions. PFC Pete is essential for grit. He keeps us on track. Amygdala Annie is great for serious danger like avoiding a rattlesnake, but Pete is really the big thinker. Annie and Pete live in different parts of your brain, as you can see here.

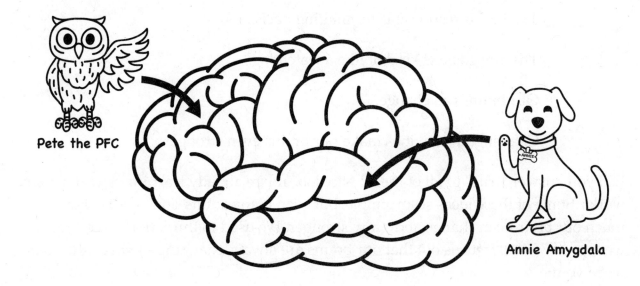

Pete the PFC

Annie Amygdala

PFC Pete is really good at helping us make changes in our brains, and it turns out that our brains change the most when we challenge ourselves. Pete actually likes it when we make mistakes and learn from them. He works so hard on learning new information that he actually makes our brain stronger. Remember Squeaker and Shaggy?

For You to Do

On the blank lines, write down whether each statement is true or false.

_____ Our brains are roughly the size of a guinea pig.

_____ The PFC is responsible for making decisions.

_____ The amygdala is kind of like a watchdog.

_____ Our brains can change.

_____ Challenging activities make our brains even stronger.

Did you answer "true" to all of these? Nice job. You're already learning how the brain works. Some of these ideas seem simple, but even many adults don't realize how much our brains can change and grow stronger. We used to think that our brains were pretty fixed. It turns out that our brains are always changing—especially when we're young.

For You to Know

Imagine that you are facing a dangerous situation: a huge orange tiger with very large teeth is running right toward you at this very second! Are you going to start working on your homework or are you going to run? *Run!*

There's a good reason you're going to start running: Amygdala Annie wants to keep you safe. She knows that homework is not as important as surviving this urgent, dangerous situation. There is no way Annie is going to let PFC Pete get involved. She will block any information from even getting to him. We aren't going to be *thoughtful* about a tiger. No. We are going to do what we need to do to survive.

When our Annies think we're in trouble, they hit our alarm buttons and start barking. All this noise and action send signals to our bodies, and those signals get our bodies ready to do one of three things:

- Fight back to protect ourselves.

- Flee from the danger … *now!*

- Freeze in place so we aren't noticed.

You may have heard of this. Some people call it the fight-or-flight response. More recently it's been called *fight, flight, or freeze* because we've noticed there's a third way to respond. Either way, it's how our brains protect us when we're facing danger.

Here's an interesting wrinkle. If we don't get enough sleep or are really hungry, our brains can overreact. It's good old Amygdala Annie who causes the overreaction. For example, if you're really tired, Annie might think, *Emma is really tired today, so she may be slow. I will help her out by OVERreacting to any possible problems. That way I will keep her safe. I will bark like crazy if anything at all happens.*

Annie is trying to help, but it's hard to function well when our brains are so jumpy. The same is true when we're hungry or don't get enough exercise: Annie gets even more protective, and she overreacts to situations that don't really need big reactions.

This is a problem because when Amygdala Annie is alarmed, she doesn't let information get to PFC Pete. She barks and runs in circles around the tree, and Pete can't see or hear what's really going on. And when Pete can't tell what's going on, he can't help us think carefully about a situation. And we need Pete's wisdom and thoughtfulness to power through.

In order to build our grit, we have to help Annie learn to relax. We need her to quiet down so PFC Pete can open his eyes and ears again. We need Pete to help us respond calmly and logically.

For You to Do

One of the best ways to get Amygdala Annie to stop barking and overreacting is pretty simple: Calm down. If you can get your body to simmer down, Amygdala Annie will also calm down, and information will be allowed to get to PFC Pete. Special types of breathing can really help Annie relax and allow PFC Pete to do his thing.

Box breathing is a technique that's especially helpful. Try it out!

1. Slowly exhale (breathe out) through your mouth. Let out all the air you can.

2. Slowly inhale (breathe in) through your nose. Count to four as you breathe in.

3. Hold your breath for four seconds.

4. Slowly exhale *through your mouth for four seconds.*

It's a little hard to do this—to breathe out slowly is hard and to breathe in slowly is hard. It might take some practice, but we know by now that you are able to do tough things! So practice.

This type of breathing actually makes your heart slow down and your blood pressure drop lower. As a result, you feel more relaxed and calm. When you're calm, Amygdala Annie cn't panic. Try to imagine Amygdala Annie slowly curling up and falling to sleep while PFC Pete stands up straight and tall, peering around with his wise eyes and ears.

Practice box breathing when you're calm and relaxed. Try when you're riding in the car, walking the dog, setting the table, or just lying in bed. The more you practice box breathing when you're calm, the easier—and more effective—it will be when you really need it.

To help you keep track of your practice, use this chart below or download a copy at http://www.newharbinger.com/45984. Try to practice three times a day (it will only take a couple of minutes!), and then check it off on the chart when you're done.

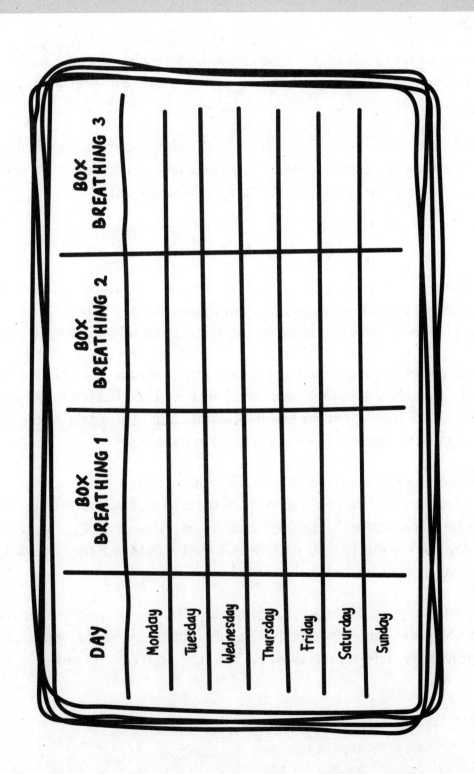

DAY	BOX BREATHING 1	BOX BREATHING 2	BOX BREATHING 3
Monday			
Tuesday			
Wednesday			
Thursday			
Friday			
Saturday			
Sunday			

Name to Tame

Ally wanted a bagel in her lunch for school. She was packing her lunch for the day, and there were no bagels in the house. Ally did not want a sandwich or soup or anything else. She wanted a bagel.

Ally started to cry. She thought, This is so unfair! Today is going to be terrible. I don't even want to go to school now! *Ally plopped down on the floor of the kitchen, unwilling to get up or move. She felt sad, angry, and disappointed.*

For You to Know

Feelings can be big and overwhelming. As you just learned, our brains react to our feelings in different ways. If we are scared, our brains may try to protect us. If we are happy, we tend to feel lighter and more active. What about other feelings?

Here is the top secret fact about feelings: *Feelings are not always true.* The truth is, feelings can lie. Not always, but feelings definitely have been known to tell some big fibs. Guess who's responsible for that happening? Yep. Amygdala Annie. Annie started barking just because there weren't bagels in the house!

Here's another example: Your mom gets mad at you for not cleaning up your room and tells you that you can't have a sleepover. You are so angry! You yell at your mom, "You always lie to me. You're the meanest mom ever!" Anger is doing the talking here, right? Are your words true? If you weren't mad, would you really be talking that way to your mom?

The first step to managing feelings is figuring out what you actually are feeling in the moment. "Name to Tame" is something a lot of therapists say to help remind kids to name their feelings. This sounds easy, but it can be pretty hard work.

For You to Do

Let's put Name to Tame into action, and name the feelings below. Read the examples, imagine how the person might be feeling, and try to figure out which of these feeling words fits the situation best: *annoyed, jealous, embarrassed, anxious,* or *furious.*

1. Lucy gets up to sharpen her pencil, and when she comes back to her desk, her friend asks if she can borrow the newly sharpened pencil to do her writing exercises.

2. Miles wants a baseball hat from his favorite team. His best friend shows up at school wearing the exact same hat he wants.

3. Tina has a major crush on a kid in her class. She writes a note to her best friend telling her about the crush. Her crush intercepts the note and reads it.

4. Ben stayed up late working on his assignment for math. He thinks that if he doesn't do well on this assignment he will never be good at math.

5. Madison takes a test in social studies. Her teacher sees her looking around the room as she thinks about her answer. Her teacher takes her into the hallway and accuses her of cheating, when she definitely was not cheating.

Answers: 1. annoyed, 2. jealous, 3. embarrassed, 4. anxious, 5. furious

Activity 10 Thoughts and Feelings: BFFs?

Diego and his friend are at lunch. His friend tells him that he got every answer correct on the spelling test that day. Diego didn't do so well on the test, and he starts to feel angry. He thinks, He's a jerk! He's trying to make me look bad! *Diego has a hard time finishing his lunch. He feels mad at his friend, and he feels embarrassed about his own score on the test.*

For You to Know

Feelings and thoughts can be BFFs, frenemies, and even enemies. Feelings tell your brain what to think, but they don't always tell the truth. Big feelings can get Amygdala Annie barking—for a reason as small as a bagel.

Here's the good news: we can change our feelings through our thoughts and our actions. Let's take this one step at a time: (1) Feelings are emotions that we experience mostly in our bodies, and (2) thoughts are words, ideas, or images that we say or think to ourselves.

The Grit Workbook for Kids

Learning to change our thoughts is one way to change our feelings. Put another way, you can learn to feel stronger and grittier by changing how you think. It will take some practice to get the hang of this, so let's get started.

For You to Do

What is a thought and what is a feeling? Circle the feeling words below:

"I am so mad at that kid!"

"He did that on purpose!"

"Now I won't get to go on the trip!"

"I am so disappointed!"

"Why can't I do anything right?"

"I wish I hadn't done that."

"I'm so scared."

"What if I can't do it?"

Did you circle "mad," "disappointed," and "scared"? Those were the feeling words in the list. But you probably realized that the thoughts listed above also show feelings. For example, "He did that on purpose" describes anger, and "I wish I hadn't done that" describes regret or shame.

Our thoughts explain our feelings in this way:

1. You *feel* something first, usually in your body. Your heart races. Your stomach flutters.

2. Your brain tries to make sense of the feeling.

3. Your brain uses *thoughts* to explain the feeling to you.

If you have trouble figuring out a feeling, the first place to look is your thoughts.

Catching Thoughts

For You to Know

We are always having thoughts! Even as you read this, you're almost certainly having them: *This is getting interesting,* for example, or *I want an apple.* It can be really hard to notice all the different thoughts that go through our minds. Noticing thoughts is especially tricky when you're trying to look for a special kind of thought called an automatic thought.

Automatic thoughts are just what they sound like: thoughts that happen automatically. They go through our mind superfast. A lot of the time we don't even notice them at all. Automatic thoughts tend to occur when we are feeling big emotions. For example, when Tricia missed the goal in a hockey game, her automatic thoughts were *I always miss the goal. I can't do anything right.* These thoughts come quickly, and unless we look for them, it is very hard to notice what they are saying. But, just like Lily and the pink cars, if we start to pay attention to them, we can start to catch them.

Why catch thoughts? Your thoughts are the way to understand feelings, especially those uncomfortable feelings you want to tame. When something happens:

We *feel* some response.

We *think* something about the response.

Our thought explains to us how we feel about what happened—but our thoughts aren't always right!

Imagine this: The TV news is on, and the broadcaster says, "Baby bunnies have escaped from a farm, and they are on the loose! They could be anywhere! They could be in your backyard right now!" You hear the announcer's deep voice, and you hear the alarm in his tone. He said there could be baby bunnies in your backyard … right *now!*

You feel scared! Amygdala Annie wakes up from a nap and starts to bark. Your thoughts are racing, and you're thinking, *Oh no! Baby bunnies … everywhere! I'm going to die!*

You exhale and begin to practice box breathing. Three breaths, four, five … Amygdala Annie falls back asleep and PFC Pete opens his eyes to see what's going on. You realize, *Hey, baby bunnies aren't scary. Baby bunnies are adorable.*

Sometimes the way something sounds makes us panic. When that happens, we need to take a step back and look at the facts. In this case, the reality is that an outbreak of baby bunnies is dangerous only to the bunnies themselves. Just because we feel something doesn't mean it's true. And just because we think something doesn't mean it's true either.

There's a special name for the type of automatic thoughts that are negative and make us feel too scared, too mad, or too bad about ourselves. They're called NATS, which stands for negative automatic thoughts. NATS are thoughts that pop into our minds without warning, and they usually make us feel bad in some way, such as scared or angry or jealous.

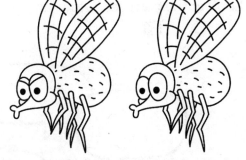

For You to Do

It can be tricky to get the hang of catching NATS. You have to pay very close attention to what's going through your mind when a situation happens. Sometimes you aren't 100 percent sure what you were thinking, and that's normal. You can go back and relook at situations and guess what your thoughts probably were. Guessing doesn't sound superscientific, but *you* are the very best expert about you. You're the best person to figure out what you would think in a situation.

Look at the pictures below, and write in the automatic thoughts you think would fit.

Miguel got new shoes for his birthday. He loved the shoes, and he couldn't wait to wear them to school the next day. Unfortunately, when he woke up that morning, it was raining. The rain stopped by recess time, but the ground was soaked. His new shoes were covered in mud within minutes. Miguel was so sad and disappointed. He thought, My shoes are ruined! This is the worst day ever!

When Miguel showed his teacher his muddy shoes, she said, "At least you have shoes. There are kids all over the world who don't even have any shoes to wear. You should feel lucky to have those shoes!"

For You to Know

Have you ever been told to think positive? Adults love to say this to kids. When Miguel's teacher told him he was lucky to have shoes, he knew it was true, but it wasn't helpful at that moment.

When we change our thoughts, we can start to change how we feel. But, we have to *believe* our thoughts in order to change them. When we change our thoughts, they have to be changed to more positive *but still realistic* thoughts. Here's an example. If Miguel's teacher had said, "That's so disappointing! I'm sorry you have mud on your new shoes. Why don't you try washing them tonight and see if you can get it out?" it probably would have been more helpful.

When Miguel's teacher told him he was lucky to have shoes, she meant well, but she was using a "rainbow unicorn" thought to try to help. Rainbow unicorn thoughts just don't work.

What are rainbow unicorn thoughts anyway? They are thoughts that are overly positive. They are the thoughts that people (usually grown-ups) tell us to think when things go wrong, because those people want us to feel better or at least get over what's bothering us. Here's an example: *I forgot my lunch, but it's okay. Being hungry today will teach me what it's like for kids who don't have enough to eat. It's actually a good thing that I forgot my lunch.*

Are you rolling your eyes? Who thinks like that? Total rainbow unicorn thought.

What's the opposite of a rainbow unicorn thought? A "crying crocodile" thought. Crying crocodile thoughts usually pop into our heads when we're down, and we have to be careful not to believe them. Crying crocodile thoughts can be very convincing. Here's the same thought but in crying crocodile form: *I forgot my lunch. I'm going to be hungry all day. I am literally going to starve. It will be a terrible day. My life is terrible.*

This crying crocodile thought is *too* terrible, and it makes everything feel much worse than it actually is.

If rainbow unicorn thoughts are simply unbelievable and crying crocodile thoughts make things seem a lot worse than they really are, how about trying to look for true and helpful thoughts? True and helpful thoughts are between rainbow unicorn and crying crocodile thoughts.

The Grit Workbook for Kids

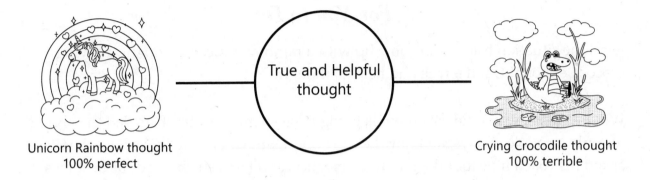

Unicorn Rainbow thought
100% perfect

True and Helpful thought

Crying Crocodile thought
100% terrible

Generally, true and helpful thoughts sound something like this: "Something went wrong, but I can get through it. I don't have to like it, but I can keep going." These thoughts are realistic *and* optimistic.

Here's the same example in true and helpful form:

I forgot my lunch. That stinks! I'd better ask my teacher for help so I won't be hungry all day.

For You to Do

Read the situation below and come up with a rainbow unicorn thought, a crying crocodile thought, and a true and helpful thought.

Will lost his new hoodie. His mom is going to be so mad at him. He's had the hoodie for only a couple of days, and now he can't find it anywhere. He looked at school, he asked his coach if he found a hoodie at practice, and he even checked his brother's drawers. He's going to be in so much trouble! And he really loved that hoodie. It was his favorite.

Rainbow unicorn thought: _____

_____

_____

Crying crocodile thought: _____

_____

_____

True and helpful thought: _____

_____

_____

Self-Talk: Yes, Talk to Yourself!

Ellie loves to draw. Ellie wants to be an artist when she grows up, and she spends all her free time doodling pictures of cute animals, beautiful flowers, and cozy houses.

Ellie is not good at drawing people yet, and she knows being able to draw people can be an important part of being an artist. Every time Ellie tries to draw a person, she thinks, That's the worst person ever! This drawing is awful! I'll never be able to draw a person!

For You to Know

These thoughts are not helpful, and they get in the way of building grit. Ellie is working on changing her thoughts to be true and helpful, but she needs a little boost. This is where self-talk comes in.

Here's how it works: Imagine you are having a hard time with something, and you want to quit or give up—*but* you also want to build your grit and keep going. It's just so hard! Wouldn't it be nice if you had your own personal coach to talk you through the hard moments? The fact is, you do! You can be your own coach, by using something called *positive self-talk*.

Don't worry, this doesn't mean we expect you to walk around your school talking to yourself out loud. No way! Self-talk is done in our heads so that no one else can hear.

Here's how Ellie used self-talk. First, she told herself, *This person isn't great, but it's better than the last person I drew.* This wasn't helping enough; she still wanted to give up. She needs some stronger self-talk techniques, so she makes a plan.

1. She imagines herself as a coach. In her imagination, she's wearing a hat and a whistle around her neck, and she's holding a notepad.

2. Next, she thinks about what a coach might say to encourage her. She comes up with true and helpful thoughts that are optimistic and encouraging.

CBT Skills to Help Kids Cultivate a Growth Mindset & Build Resilience

3. Then she practices saying those things to herself. She practices them in her head when she's drawing. Sometimes she also practices them in front of a mirror when she's alone.

4. Last, when she's talking to herself, Ellie uses her own name. (Research shows this makes us listen more closely.)

Here's what Ellie ended up saying to herself:

Ellie, you can already draw lots of things.
There's no reason you can't learn to draw a person.

Ellie, take your time, and make mistakes,
but keep going. Ellie, you can do this.

Ellie, you are able to do hard things! Remember
how hard it was to draw a koala? You figured it out.
You'll figure this out too.

For You to Do

Read the examples below and circle the words or sentences that show helpful self-talk in action.

Abby, you are doing a terrible job! This is not working at all! Do better!

Ben, what were you thinking? This is a mess. You can't do anything right!

This is really hard to do, but you are able to do hard things. Keep going, Eva!

Spencer, of course you want to quit, but you don't have to quit. You can keep going.

You probably had no trouble figuring out which words and sentences were helpful and which were not. One way to know is by how they make you feel. Helpful self-talk makes you feel like you can keep going; words that make you feel hopeless or bad about yourself do just the opposite.

More to Do

Let's think about a time when you wanted to give up on something. We all have moments like that. Now imagine yourself as a coach. Got the image? Good. What would you want your self-talk coach to have said to you? What might have helped? Write in your answers below and remember to include your name in the self-talk!

The situation: _____

_____

_____

What your self-talk coach said to you: _____

_____

_____

Tommy had to present his science project to his class, and he was nervous. He hated talking in front of the whole class, and he was sure he was going to do something to embarrass himself. He had a hard time sleeping the night before the presentation, and the next morning he felt sick to his stomach. He thought the information he had to show them was pretty cool, and he wanted to share what he had learned with his classmates, but he wasn't sure he could do it.

For You to Know

Sometimes we need to use more than one tool, or *strategy*, in order to stick with something and push through the difficulty. Being your own coach is one excellent strategy. Another is one we'll call motivation mantras.

Our desire to keep going is called *motivation*, and gritty kids know how to motivate themselves to do hard things. Motivation is the reason that we want to do something. Tommy has used his other grit strategies, but now he wants to have a grit tool he can literally carry in his pocket. This tool is something simple and helpful that he can use in the moments of big stress right before the presentation.

He decides to create a *mantra*. A mantra is a word or sentence that we repeat out loud or in our heads to calm and focus ourselves when we are seriously stressed. People often think mantras are just for meditation or yoga, but they can be used in any situation.

For You to Do

Think back to the past year. Remember two or three accomplishments that you are really proud of. These could have happened during the school year or during the summer break. Write those accomplishments below.

Accomplishment 1: _____

_____

_____

Accomplishment 2: _____

_____

_____

Accomplishment 3: _____

_____

_____

What makes you most proud of these accomplishments? How did you show grit in achieving them? Write a sentence or two describing both your pride and your grit.

_____

_____

_____

_____

Ready for your mantra? Look back at what you wrote above, and decide on a simple sentence that summarizes your motivation and grit. You can use the ideas that follow, or you can create your own.

- I am strong and capable.

- I can do hard things.

- I keep going.

- I am capable.

- I don't give up easily.

- I can handle being uncomfortable.

Write your personal mantra in the box below. You can memorize this mantra, and you can also write it on a piece of paper to carry in your pocket. Either way, you'll always have it with you.

The Three Ps

Katy wakes up every morning thinking it's going to be a good day. She smiles at her parents, she looks forward to going to school—she's just an optimistic kid. During breakfast, Katy chats with her parents about what's going to happen that day at school, and she focuses on the parts she's most looking forward to. She talks about her upcoming art class, and how she hopes the cafeteria has the really good pizza for lunch.

Emily refuses to get out of bed when her alarm goes off. She snaps at her parents, and she dreads school. Emily is more of a pessimistic kid. When Emily's parents try to talk with her during breakfast, she reminds them that she is "not a morning person" and asks them to please be quiet. Her thoughts focus on the drama that happened at lunch yesterday, and she starts to dread the whole day.

For You to Know

Both Katy and Emily are awesome kids. They are supercool, nice, and fun to be around. But there's no doubt that Katy has it easier. We call Katy an optimist, but it's really Katy's *thoughts* that are optimistic. Katy thinks in a way that means she sees things happier and brighter.

An optimist is a person who chooses to stay hopeful and positive about life, even when life isn't exactly going their way. Have you ever heard the expression that a glass is either "half full" or "half empty"? In this example, the glass is filled up to the middle, but you get to choose how you see it: half full or half empty? Katy, an optimist, would say it's half full. Emily, a pessimist, might say it's half empty. (Both are true, but remember, you get to *choose* how you see it.)

The Grit Workbook for Kids

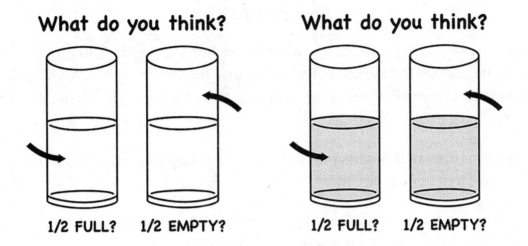

Gritty kids choose to think more optimistically. They decide to see a situation in a positive but true and helpful way.

For You to Do

To become more positive you have to learn to catch those negative automatic thoughts and change them. A famous teacher and researcher named Dr. Martin Seligman found there are three types of thoughts that make us think more negatively.

He calls these types of thoughts the "three Ps." The thoughts are *permanent, pervasive,* and *personal.* Here's what they mean.

1. *Permanent.* You believe that things will never change, never get better. It will always be this way. An example of a permanent thought is "I overreact to everything. I will always be this way." Permanent thoughts are like big, solid boulders. They seem like they will be there forever.

2. *Pervasive.* This means your thoughts reflect every single part of your life. If one thing goes wrong, then everything is ruined: "I was the last one chosen for kickball; no one wants to be with me." When our thoughts are pervasive, it's like everything in our life gets affected. Imagine if you burned a tray of

cookies. The bad smell would go throughout your house, and it would even stick to your clothes. Pervasive thoughts impact all parts of your life.

3. *Personal.* You caused it, or it's about you. If you don't get invited to a birthday party, it's because you did something wrong or you are not likable: "Those kids are whispering, and I think they looked over at me. They must be talking about me." When we have personal thoughts, we assume way too much. And our assumptions tend to hurt us. Look at this picture; personal thoughts make it all about us in a way that is too big and usually untrue.

Draw a line from each thought to the correct P: permanent, pervasive, or personal.

	Permanent
Julie hates me! She thinks I'm awful.	Pervasive
	Personal
	Permanent
I failed the test. I will never learn how to do this math.	Pervasive
	Personal
	Permanent
My mom is mad at me. This is going to be a terrible weekend.	Pervasive
	Personal
	Permanent
The teacher canceled the party. The whole class is miserable.	Pervasive
	Personal

58

The Grit Workbook for Kids

I'm the only one who failed the quiz. There's something wrong with me.	Permanent Pervasive Personal
I am the slowest kid in my class. I will always finish last in PE races.	Permanent Pervasive Personal

If you had trouble deciding which P any of the thoughts are, you are not alone. Even if you got some wrong, it's okay. Remember, our brain learns even better when we make mistakes and then correct them. Every time you learn from a mistake, you build grit!

More to Do

Now that you have been introduced to the three Ps, let's try to catch some P thoughts in your own life. Pay attention to your thoughts, and add a couple of thoughts each day to the categories that best describe them. You can use the form that follows, or download a copy at http://www.newharbinger.com/45984.

This is a good activity to have a grown-up help you complete because it can be hard to remember to write the thoughts down. It's also tricky to learn which of the three Ps best fits.

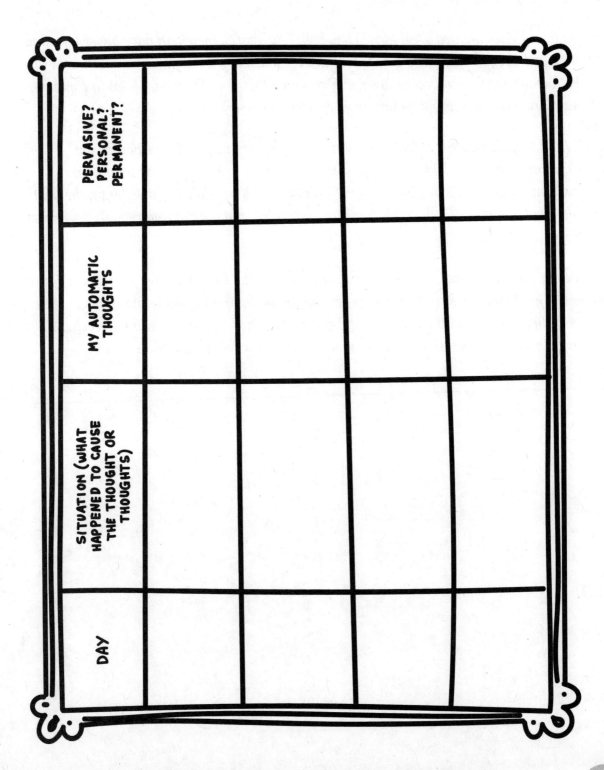

DAY	SITUATION (WHAT HAPPENED TO CAUSE THE THOUGHT OR THOUGHTS)	MY AUTOMATIC THOUGHTS	PERVASIVE? PERSONAL? PERMANENT?

Growth Thinking

Paul and Zack are two great kids. They both love sports, they both have big sisters, and they both love to play video games on the weekend. They know they are smart, and they both want to get good grades to show how smart they are. They have a lot in common, but they also have very different ways of seeing the world.

When Paul doesn't get a good grade on a test, he gets mad at his teacher for not explaining the material well enough, or he blames the kid sitting next to him for breathing too loud during the test. Instead of figuring out how to do better on the next test, Paul hopes his teacher gets better at explaining and his classmates make less noise next time.

When Zack gets a bad grade on a test, he looks at what he did wrong. He tries to figure out if he should have studied harder or if he should have asked more questions because he didn't understand the material well enough. Zack asks to meet with the teacher to go over the answers he missed, and he makes sure he learns the material.

For You to Know

A famous researcher named Carol Dweck has spent her whole career studying an idea called *mindset.* Dr. Dweck has found that people have two main types of mindsets: fixed and growth.

A fixed mindset is a belief that people are born the way they are. Just like some people have brown eyes and some people have blue eyes, some people are born smart and some people are not. Paul's mindset is pretty fixed in the example, isn't it? He doesn't seem to think there's anything he can do on his own to get a better grade. His beliefs are fixed, kind of like a padlock.

Zack is a kid with more of a growth mindset. He believes that natural talent is really nice, but you don't have to be born talented to get good at something. He also sees failures and mistakes as opportunities to learn new stuff and get better. Zack's beliefs are all about growth. His growth mindset is like a growing plant.

Kids who believe they can do well if they work hard have an easier time when life gets tough. Why is this? The truth is, it matters what you *think*. Having a growth mindset makes it easier to do all kinds of things simply because you believe you can do them.

For You to Do

Even if you don't have a growth mindset right now, you can learn to build up that skill. The first step is to learn the difference between growth mindset thoughts and fixed mindset thoughts. Below is a list of thoughts some kids have. Cross out the "fixed" ones. Circle the "growth" ones.

I'm bad at math.

I'm not good at sports.

Swimming isn't my thing.

I can do well on the test if I study.

I can do better if I work at it.

I'm terrible at gymnastics!

I'll get better at playing guitar if I practice.

I can learn new things if I try.

This homework is too hard for me!

I can do this if I break it down into steps.

I'm a terrible cook!

I'll keep trying and see what happens.

Talk about your answers with a friend or a grown-up. It's okay if you didn't get some right. Talking it over with someone else can help you think and learn about your mindset. And, while you're learning, you're building your grit.

Pete has a baby brother, Tommy, who is just learning to walk. Tommy is not very good at walking. In fact, he seems to fall most of the time. Tommy doesn't give up, though. He keeps practicing and practicing until he can walk well.

For You to Know

When we get older, we start to become more aware of the possibility of success or failure. Because we know it's possible we might fail, we see greater risk in a situation than a baby does. This is good, because it stops us from doing dangerous things. It can also be a problem, though, because the fear of failing at something stops us from trying.

Growth mindsets are all about knowing that you if want to succeed, you have to work at it. Kids with growth mindsets often think about how they are able to learn and how their brains can get stronger. These kids still face challenges. In fact, one of the skills of having a growth mindset is knowing there will be obstacles, and that those obstacles need to be faced to move forward. Learning from obstacles actually strengthens your grit. Hiding from obstacles or quitting when things get tough, on the other hand, makes a fixed mindset stronger.

For You to Do

Imagine you are taking a very hard test at school. As you're reading over the test, you realize you studied the wrong information! What do you imagine you would think? Write those thoughts in this bubble.

If you're like most of us, your first thought was probably a fixed mindset thought. Maybe it was something like: *I can't do this! I'm sure she didn't teach us this material! I'm going to fail.* That's okay. Once you learn to recognize these thoughts for what they are, you can learn to change them.

The Grit Workbook for Kids

Let's practice changing fixed mindset thoughts into growth mindset thoughts. First, was your thought a fixed mindset thought or a growth mindset thought?

_____

If it was a fixed mindset thought, then try changing it to a growth mindset thought. Write your new thought in this bubble.

Not so hard, right? You are on your way to building a strong growth mindset.

Activity 18 Grateful for Gratitude

For You to Know

Kids who are grateful, who focus on the things they have instead of the things they don't have, tend to be happier. This isn't always easy to do. Our brains are really good at getting us to think about everything we want, instead of helping us focus on everything we have.

In order to be grateful for something or someone, we have to decide to be grateful. Sound confusing? Gratitude, like grit, is a choice. We choose gratitude by deliberately noticing awesome moments, by paying attention to our feelings, and by acknowledging good and kind acts by others.

Here's an example: Your soccer team finally wins a game, and you are so grateful for winning. Winning the soccer game wasn't a gift to you, but the hard work of the team was. You feel grateful for the awesome defense work by the goalie, the pass your friend made to you midway through the game, and the cheering by your dad and sister, which really boosted your morale.

Research shows gratitude works best when we are grateful for something specific. If you think to yourself, *I'm grateful for everyone in the whole world,* well, that's a really nice thought—but it's kind of a rainbow unicorn thought, isn't it? It would matter more to you if you thought, *I'm grateful to my mom and dad for reading me my favorite books at bedtime.* See the difference? Getting specific is key.

For You to Do

Catching specific moments that bring us joy, contentment, and other positive feelings is how we grow our gratitude. Writing down those specific moments when we are grateful actually makes us feel happier.

A gratitude journal is a fun way to keep track of specific moments when you feel grateful. You can use a journal of your own, copy the form below, or download it at http://www.newharbinger.com/45984.

Try to write around the same time each day to make a habit of it. Make sure you are specific with your moments of gratitude. ("When I was riding my bike down the hill, and it felt so fast and fun," rather than "Riding a bike.")

DAILY GRATITUDE JOURNAL

*BE SPECIFIC WITH ENTRIES

1

ONE MOMENT I WAS GRATEFUL FOR TODAY WAS:

_____

_____

_____

2

ONE EXPERIENCE I WAS GRATEFUL FOR TODAY WAS:

_____

_____

_____

3

I WAS GRATEFUL TODAY WHEN:

_____

_____

_____

It can take a couple of weeks to get into the hang of using your gratitude journal. By tuning your attention to the gratitude channel, your brain starts to pick up more and more moments that feel good.

Your Shoes or Mine?

Riley's favorite shoes are his baseball cleats. He loves the sound they make when he walks across the parking lot, and he loves the way they feel when he runs on the field. When he puts them on and laces them up, he feels like an athlete: tall, strong, and confident. He starts to see things like a baseball player sees things, and he thinks like an athlete.

When Riley puts on his flip-flops, he feels a little different. He doesn't have the same burst of confidence and energy, but he doesn't feel bad either. He feels comfortable and relaxed. He likes the thwack thwack *sound the shoes make when he walks, and they take only two seconds to put on.*

 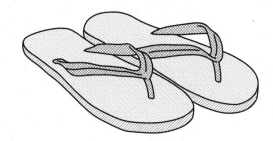

For You to Know

Why do we care about Riley's shoes? Because he feels different in different shoes. If we imagine him in his baseball cleats, we can see him in a bright uniform, standing tall. If we imagine him in his flip-flops, we can see him casually walking in the sand. Riley sees things differently in those situations too. When he is wearing his cleats, he sees the world as a baseball player. This is Riley's perspective. *Perspective* means how we see, think, and feel about a situation.

Different people have different perspectives. For example, if you noticed a squirrel in the backyard you might think, *That squirrel is so cute!* But your mom, who has been working in her garden, might think, *That squirrel is terrible! It's trying to eat all my plants!* If your dog could tell you its thoughts, it might be thinking, *I want to chase that squirrel!* You are each looking at the same squirrel, but you each have a different perspective.

When we think about perspective, it's important to realize we all see things differently. It's easy (or at least tempting) to believe that someone else's perspective is wrong, and ours is right. Sometimes we are right! But sometimes we are wrong. And sometimes there is no right or wrong. When we learn to think about things from someone else's perspective, we get to see the situation in a different way.

For You to Do

Do you have any special shoes? Maybe they're ballet slippers or athletic shoes like Riley's cleats. Maybe you have a pair of fancy dress shoes that you wear only for special occasions. You might have a pair of the softest, coziest slippers ever, or you might have tall boots that clomp loudly on the floor when you walk in them. Go find those shoes, put them on, and take a few steps.

Which shoes did you choose? _____

Why? _____

What looks different when you put these shoes on? _____

_____

What feels different when you put these shoes on? _____

_____

What thoughts come into your mind when you're walking around in these shoes?

_____

More to Do

Ask someone in your family if they have a pair of special shoes, a pair of shoes that make them feel different and have a different perspective. Ask them to try on the shoes, and then ask them the same questions you answered above. Write their answers below.

Which shoes did you choose? _____

Why? _____

What looks different when you put these shoes on? _____

_____

What feels different when you put these shoes on? _____

_____

What thoughts come into your mind when you're walking around in these shoes?

_____

Activity 20 Lights, Camera, Action!

For You to Know

Actors are usually really good at understanding perspective. It's actually part of their job. Actors play characters. Characters are people. For actors to play a character, they have to understand how that character thinks about things, what the character believes and loves and hates, and so on. Actors study the *perspective* of their characters so they can act like them.

Think of your favorite actor. Have you seen that person in only one role? Probably not. If they are famous, you've probably seen them playing several different roles. Maybe they were a villain in one show and a hero in the next. In each role, the actor probably spent weeks or even months thinking about the perspective of those different characters.

How do actors learn to think like someone else? They try to see and understand things the same way their character does. Actors literally step into someone else's shoes, using three steps.

- *Curiosity.* Curiosity is a perspective superpower. If you are curious about someone else, you start to wonder about how they live, their interests and beliefs, and how they might think about a situation. You also might start to wonder: *Why did she do that?* or *What was she thinking about?* or *What were her parents like?*

- *Imagining.* Imagining helps you start to get a picture of someone as more than just the person you see right now. The person you see right now probably has a mom, maybe has a dog, could have a sister; they may live on a llama farm or a houseboat on the ocean. When you imagine the details of that person's life, they start to become more real.

- *Recognizing similarities.* Sometimes actors don't like their characters or have a hard time connecting to the character. When this happens, they look for things they have in common with the character. It's easy to think about how different we are from other people, but we can understand perspective more when we see our similarities. The character may share your love of Jell-O, pistachio ice cream, or olives. They may also like your favorite TV show, book, or movie. You probably have some things in common with this character. Find the similarities and name them to help you see through this person's eyes.

For You to Do

Are you ready to become an actor? We're going to give you a pretend role in a pretend movie. Ready?

You are a ten-year-old who was born in New York City. When you were one, your family moved to a farm in Connecticut. You don't remember living in the city at all. You love living in the country. All your free time is spent playing outside. You have an older and a younger sister, and they are your best friends. The three of you play together all the time. You have a dog named Rascal, who never leaves your side. You live with both your parents. Your mom is a science teacher at the local school, and your dad is a librarian.

To get started, ask yourself:

1. What are you curious about?

2. What do you wonder about this kid?

3. How do you imagine this kid's life?

Here are your lines; try to say them in the "voice" of your character.

Line 1: "I am so excited to move back to the city. I can't wait to see all the tall buildings. I love the noise of cars and buses."

Line 2: "I can't believe that my parents signed me up for a different activity every single day of the week."

Line 3: "I just want to be outside. I just want to breathe fresh air. I miss Rascal."

How did it go? Were you able to stay curious, wonder, and imagine how the character thought, felt, and acted? What did you notice while you read your lines?

_____

_____

_____

Perspective Check

Kyra is tired. She didn't sleep enough last night, and she wakes up in a bad mood. She wants to stay in bed, and her parents get mad at her for not getting up on time. Her mom makes her rush to get ready for school, and she can't find the shirt she wanted to wear. She finally finds it in her sister's room. She's so mad at her sister for borrowing her shirt without asking! When she's finally ready to leave, her mom is mad because she took too long, and she rushes Kyra out the door—into pouring rain.

Kyra gets a tardy at school that day, and she feels embarrassed. She has science first thing in the morning, and when she opens her folder to find her homework, she realizes she left it at home. Kyra starts to cry. She feels awful! She goes to the bathroom so no one will see her crying.

She thinks, This is so unfair! My life is terrible! Nothing ever works out for me. I'll probably fail this grade. I'll probably have to miss recess to do the homework. My teacher will never believe I actually did it. *At this moment, everything seems absolutely miserable.*

For You to Know

Kyra isn't alone. We've all had times when we get completely overwhelmed and just lose it. When life isn't going your way, or when you're faced with lots of things going wrong, it's easy to feel like everything is terrible. You probably feel discouraged and down. Your feelings seem to grow bigger, and at the same time, the situation starts to feel much worse than it really is.

When we're in the middle of feeling terrible, it usually feels like it will always be this way. But that's not the case at all. The fact is, feelings are temporary. Just as you can't be happy forever, you can't feel upset forever either. It's like the weather. When a big thunderstorm is rolling through, it seems like the whole world is dark and wet—but that storm will end. Feelings always end too.

Sometimes these big feelings can cause us to lose perspective. In other words, those feelings cause us to see a situation differently from how it really is. When this happens, we have to get our perspective back. We need to *keep* our perspective.

Keeping perspective means taking a step back to look at things in a way that is based on facts and evidence—how things really are. When everything feels terrible, it's very hard to remember there are many ways to view the situation. Learning to do something called a *perspective check* can help. Perspective checks can help you see that good things can still happen, and that everything might be okay after all.

For You to Do

A perspective check is a way to see the situation more accurately. To practice, think about a time you may have lost your perspective in the past week. You couldn't find your homework anywhere, and you actually accused your dog of eating it. Or you hated your dinner and told your dad it was terrible and there was no way you would eat it. If you can't think of one in the past week, then use Kyra's situation and try to think about how she might answer these questions:

- How big a deal will this be in two hours?

- How big a deal will this be in two days?

- Why is it important to remember that feelings are *temporary*?

Check your perspective any time you need to by writing down these questions so you can have them with you at home, at school, or wherever you are. That way, you'll be able to ask yourself the questions whenever your feelings start to feel too big. (Reminder to self: Just because this feels true doesn't mean it is. What are the facts?)

When you first start doing perspective checks, they can be very tough to complete. Stick with it. It gets easier and easier the more you practice. Most kids find that after a couple of weeks of practicing the perspective check, they use it automatically when they're going through difficult moments. And, when you get in the habit of doing perspective checks, you build grit. Grit requires you to keep going when you want to give up and to stick with things that are hard. When you have a better sense of perspective, you can use that knowledge to see things as they really are, not just how they feel. This knowledge allows you to think differently about a situation, and to choose to keep going when you might want to just give up.

More to Do

Write a note to Kyra that you think might help her feel better. As you're writing the letter, think about what you wish people would have said to you when you were struggling and couldn't see your way out.

Dear Kyra

Activity 22

What's the Problem?

Alex is struggling with learning his multiplication tables. He just can't seem to memorize the numbers well, and he's starting to dread math class. Whenever it's time to share his times tables out loud, he goes to the bathroom so no one will realize how much he's struggling. One day, his teacher lets him know that she would like to offer him extra help because she knows he's having a hard time. Alex doesn't go for extra help, and he gets more and more worried. He actually gets a stomachache before school on the day of the multiplication quiz, and he stays home from school. Alex thinks his teacher is disappointed in him, and he doesn't want his parents to know how badly he is doing in math because he thinks they will be mad.

For You to Know

Like Alex, we all have problems that we don't know how to solve. Sometimes a problem can be so hard we don't even know where to get started. When this happens, gritty kids start by identifying the problem. This may sound simple, but it's not always as easy as it sounds. This is especially true when there's more than one possible problem!

For You to Do

So what is Alex's problem here? Circle the ones that you think fit. There can be more than one.

He has a hard time learning multiplication tables.

He dreads math class.

He isn't studying or practicing multiplication tables.

His teacher is disappointed in him.

His parents will be mad if they find out how badly he is doing.

Okay, now we've got at least one problem and probably some other problems too. Look back at the ones you circled, and rank them in order from easiest to fix to hardest to fix.

By identifying which problems are the easiest, you also are recognizing which are the most fixable. If a problem seems completely unfixable, we tend to back away and give up. But, if we can change our perspective and look at the problem differently, we have a better chance of being able to solve the problem. If we start with the easiest problems, we realize that they are fixable.

For example, if you think your teacher is the nicest person in the whole world, you probably ranked "His teacher is disappointed in him" higher than someone who thinks their teacher is not that great. In other words, the more you care about your teacher, the more you would care if they were disappointed in you.

More to Do

After you identify the problem, the next step is to make a plan. How are you going to solve Alex's problem?

Clearly define the problem. Be specific.

What are a couple of possible solutions?

Which solution do you want to try first? Why?

When are you going to try it, and how often are you going to work on it?

PROBLEM-SOLVING PLAN

· 1 ·

CLEARLY DEFINE
THE PROBLEM.
BE SPECIFIC.

· 2 ·

WHAT ARE
A COUPLE OF POSSIBLE
SOLUTIONS?

· 3 ·

WHICH SOLUTION
DO YOU WANT
TO TRY FIRST? WHY?

· 4 ·

WHEN ARE YOU GOING
TO TRY IT, AND HOW OFTEN
ARE YOU GOING TO
WORK ON IT?

Do You SEE!

Jack stayed up way too late playing on his mom's iPad. The next morning he was tired and grumpy, and he barely managed to eat a quick bowl of sugar puff cereal before dragging himself out to catch the bus. Jack and his friend were working on a project about Ancient Greece in school that day, and what do you think happened when Jack's friend made a mistake on the paper? Yep, you guessed it—Jack got angry and lost his perspective. He called his friend stupid and stormed out of the classroom without permission.

For You to Know

One of the first steps to growing your grit is to give your brain and your body the care they need. A seed grows best when it's planted in rich soil, has plenty of sunlight, and gets just enough water. Grit grows best when your brain and your body get the care they need. If you want to SEE your grit grow, just follow the letters:

- **S**leep from nine to ten hours a night.

- **E**xercise your body to help your brain work best.

- **E**at well, including lots of fresh fruit, veggies, and protein.

Do You SEE!

For You to Do

Let's try using the SEE strategy with Jack. After each sentence below, write in what you think would have helped Jack practice SEEing more clearly. (Remember, SEE stands for Sleep, Exercise, and Eating well.)

What problems do you see with this first sentence? Jack stayed up way too late playing on his mom's iPad.

_____

_____

The next morning he was tired and grumpy, and he barely managed to eat a quick bowl of sugar puff cereal before dragging himself out to catch the bus. What do you see as the problem?

_____

_____

Staying up late and using electronics is not good for your brain and body. Kids your age need more than nine hours of sleep a night to feel their best. And using electronics right before bed is a definite no. Scientists have found all kinds of problems with the light from the devices getting in the way of good sleep. Plus, the ways our brains respond to the information on the device itself can keep us awake. Electronics shouldn't be used at all for at least two hours before bed.

Remember what fuels our brains and bodies best? Is it sugar puffs? Nope. Our brains and bodies work best when we eat high-quality foods, such as fruit, vegetables, and protein.

CBT Skills to Help Kids Cultivate a Growth Mindset & Build Resilience

More to Do

Do you want to test out this idea? Do you want to SEE if sleep, exercise, and eating well make a difference in your mood and your level of grit? You can use the chart below to track how well you SEE this week.

DAY	HOW MANY HOURS OF SLEEP DID I GET LAST NIGHT?	HOW MANY MINUTES OF EXERCISE DID I GET TODAY?	DID I EAT FRUIT, VEGETABLES, AND PROTEIN TODAY?	HOW DO I FEEL TODAY? 1-10 1=WORST AND 10=BEST	WHAT'S MY GRIT LEVEL? 1-10 (USE GRIT THERMOMETER)
Monday					
Tuesday					
Wednesday					
Thursday					
Friday					
Saturday					
Sunday					

Did you learn anything after keeping track of how well you SEE? One kid we know kept track of how much he slept, exercised, and ate for a week. He was surprised to learn that it made a big difference if he got exercise each day. He didn't want to do serious exercise each day, so he tried different strategies. He found that walking his dog with his dad and playing tag at recess really helped him feel better and sleep better. That made his grit level start to go up—and he was having fun!

Grit in Motion

For You to Know

Exercise not only helps your body, it also helps your brain. It gets your blood flowing, makes your mood better, enhances your memory, and even helps you solve problems more effectively. Scientists have found that kids who exercise do better on tests, act with more confidence, and report feeling happier.

After reading that, it probably won't surprise you to learn that exercise and grit go together as well as peanut butter and jelly. Grit takes work, and exercise is great at helping build grit because it helps kids (and grown-ups) have more energy to do that work. Did you know there are even studies showing that exercise makes people worry less? All people, not just kids, need to have their brains in tip-top shape if they are to keep at it when the going gets tough. Taking care of your body helps take care of your brain—and grows your grit.

For You to Do

Does exercise really help your mood? Let's test out this idea.

1. Use the feelings thermometer to rate your current mood.

2. Set a timer for sixty seconds, and do as many jumping jacks as you can in that period of time.

3. Set the timer for fifteen seconds and take a break.

4. Set the timer for sixty seconds, and again do as many jumping jacks as you can.

5. Quickly rate your mood again right after you finish the second round of jumping jacks.

Feelings Thermometer

10. Ahhh!!!
9. Freaking out!
8. Very bad!
7. Bad!
6. This is hard!
5. Not good.
4. A little uncomfortable.
3. Could be worse.
2. Okay, fine.
1. Good. All is well.

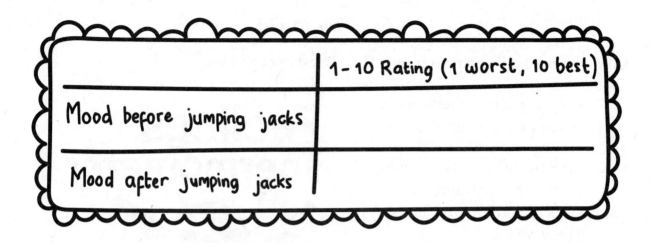

	1- 10 Rating (1 worst, 10 best)
Mood before jumping jacks	
Mood after jumping jacks	

What did you notice from this quick experiment? Put on your white lab coat, and make your notes here.

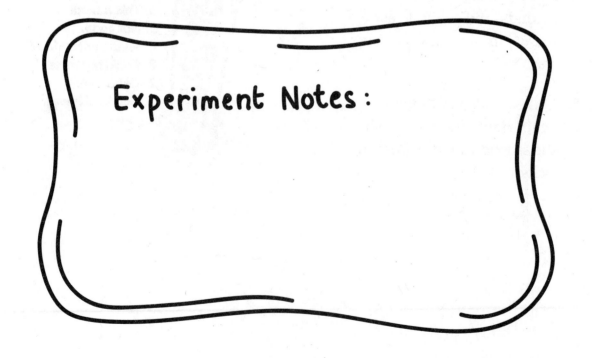

Experiment Notes :

More to Do

Let's try this again to see how exercise can affect mood *and* grit. Have a grown-up time you doing this maze.

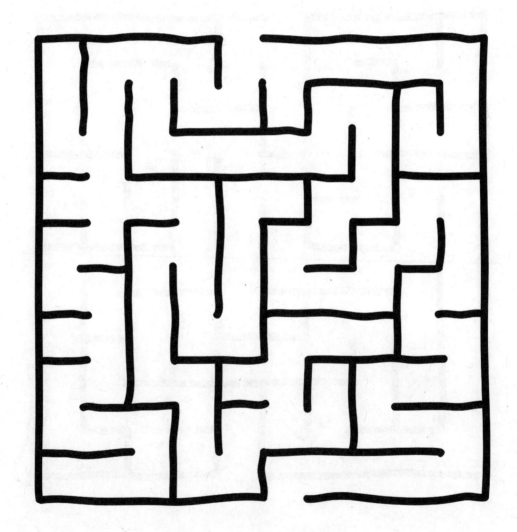

How long did it take? Write down your time: _____.

Now, have your grown-up time you as you do jumping jacks for sixty seconds, take a break for fifteen seconds, and then do sixty more seconds of jumping jacks. As soon as you're done, sit down and try this maze. Again, have a grown-up time you.

How long did it take? Write down your time: _____.

You were probably faster completing the maze exercise after you did the jumping jacks. Your brain was working more effectively and was better able to solve the problems. Isn't that cool? Doing regular exercise is important for building grit, but sometimes even short bursts of exercise can help our brains work better. When the brain is at its best, it's not just thinking and solving problems faster. It's also calmer, better able to keep perspective, and able to problem solve more effectively.

Recharge!

Charlotte loved to be busy. She liked hanging out with friends, playing on a travel sports team, being with her Girl Scout troop, taking an art class, and working hard in school. These were all great things, but Charlotte found herself feeling tired. She was stressed and irritable because she just couldn't keep up with everything. Every weeknight involved one activity after another, and her weekends were just as busy!

Charlotte's mom suggested that she start giving herself time with nothing special to do. Her mom explained that Charlotte might have to give up something from her busy schedule to make this free time, and that would be okay. Charlotte agreed, and she found some ways to cut back on her activities. She began playing outside with her dog more. She even took time to lie on the grass and stare up at the sky. It felt so good. She started reading books just for fun, and that felt good, too. She still enjoyed lots of activities, but she found that if she did a little less she had more time to recharge.

For You to Know

It takes energy to keep going when things get tough. We've already learned that getting enough sleep, eating well, and exercising give you energy—and there's even more. Having time to yourself to relax and have fun can actually give you energy too! Taking time for yourself can help boost your grit because it gives your mind and body a chance to unwind and loosen up.

Relaxing doesn't have to mean lying in bed or sitting on the couch, although sometimes it can. The fact is, doing something (versus doing nothing) can be relaxing. But it matters what the "something" is. Lots of kids say they feel more relaxed when they play games on their devices or watch videos. That can be fun in the moment, but it's not the kind of relaxation that builds grit. Scientists have studied kids using screens, and they learned that electronics make it hard for your brain to relax. Worse, electronic use can actually take your energy away and make you feel irritated and less able to concentrate and focus.

Scientists also tell us that being outside can be a great way to build up your energy. Being in nature makes kids feel less stressed. It can be super relaxing to spend time outdoors—on the playground, in a park, or in your own backyard.

For You to Do

Here are some ways kids like to relax and recharge:

- hula hooping
- drawing or painting
- meditating
- listening to music
- singing
- running
- skateboarding
- making a craft project

- playing an instrument
- spending quiet time alone
- reading
- shooting hoops
- bike-riding
- dancing
- playing with a friend
- just having fun

What have we forgotten? Add your own "recharge" ideas here.

_____

_____

_____

Which are your top three ways to recharge? List them here.

1. _____

2. _____

3. _____

Write down when you can schedule time to recharge. _____

If you can't find time for recharging but you feel stressed a lot, maybe it's time to talk with your parents about clearing some space in your busy schedule.

Sound silly? We totally understand, but sometimes we have to make a real effort to recharge. Maybe you and your parents can schedule time to recharge together (we bet they could use a little recharge time themselves—most parents can).

More to Do

How charged are you? It can be easy to start to lose charge without even noticing. It's funny, but we often know more about the charge level in our devices than we do in ourselves. Use this chart to track your charge level for the week. Fill in the battery at the same time each day and write the time on the chart. This is a fun activity to do with your parents. Feel free to add sentences that show if you are more or less charged.

· CHARGE LEVEL ·

 THINGS THAT GAVE ME A CHARGE? :)

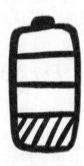 THINGS THAT DRAINED MY CHARGE? :(

- - - - - - - - - - - -

DAY   100% _____
        75% _____
        50% _____
        25% _____

DAY   100% _____
        75% _____
        50% _____
        25% _____

DAY   100% _____
        75% _____
        50% _____
        25% _____

DAY   100% _____
        75% _____
        50% _____
        25% _____

DAY   100% _____
        75% _____
        50% _____
        25% _____

DAY   100% _____
        75% _____
        50% _____
        25% _____

Tuning In

Louis is a serious cello player. He practices every day, sometimes for an hour at a time. The first thing he does when he sits down to play is tune his instrument. Tuning the cello means he makes sure the sound is right. If the cello is playing too high, he makes the sound lower. If the pitch is off, he fixes it through listening and changing the tightness of the strings. If Louis starts playing before he has tuned his instrument, it won't sound right and will mess up the song. Tuning is the first step to playing.

For You to Know

Mindfulness is a tool to help your mind work a little better, just like Louis tunes his cello to make it sound better. Mindfulness is a way of focusing your attention so that you are truly paying attention to something. When you are mindful, you are fully focused on the moment you're in and the experience you're having. It's like pressing the "pause" button and focusing only on what is around you here and now.

Kids have to do a lot in a day: go to school, do homework, and help out at home—and that doesn't even include all their activities! Cultivating a sense of mindfulness can make it easier to focus on important things. Mindfulness can also make it easier to focus on your grit because it helps you tune your attention away from the past and the future and back to this very moment. The one right now.

Being mindful does not mean ignoring problems, pretending everything is okay, or ignoring your feelings. Being mindful actually means experiencing all those things head-on.

For You to Do

Mindfulness is related to perception. When we choose to be mindful, we choose to see things as they really are. Let's test out this idea.

First, stand up and set a timer for twenty seconds. Use that twenty seconds to think about whatever you want. You could think about school, friends, the weather. Anything at all. Just stand still and think for twenty seconds, and then answer these questions.

What was it like? _____

_____

What did you think about? _____

_____

How relaxing was it? Circle one: a little   medium   very relaxing

Now, let's try the same exercise, only let's do it *mindfully*. Set your timer for twenty seconds, and then stand up tall and place your feet firmly on the ground. Try to feel the ground under your feet, and let your feet evenly touch the floor. Focus on your breathing, how grounded your legs feel, the movement in your arms. When you start to think about different things in the past or future, pull your thoughts back to right now: to your feet solidly on the ground, your arms, your legs, your breathing. Just notice what that is like, and then answer these questions.

What was it like? _____

_____

What did you think about? _____

_____

How relaxing was it? Circle one: a little   medium   very relaxing

Was the second exercise more relaxing? Someone watching you may have thought you were doing the same thing in both exercises, because from the outside they look pretty much the same. But they probably felt quite different.

Mindfulness is something you can have with you all the time. When you start to get overwhelmed, when feelings of stress start to take over, practice rooting yourself in this very moment. It is an easy and relaxing way to settle your mind and body.

Macy has a hard time focusing on things around her when she feels stressed or overwhelmed. She gets mad quickly, and she has a hard time calming herself down. Macy wants to build her grit, but sometimes it's hard to focus on grit when the world around her is so busy, distracting, and noisy. She needs a way to calm her mind and body when things get to be too much.

For You to Know

Grounding is a technique Macy can learn to use when her head is spinning. Picture a giant tree with roots that go deep into the ground, keeping the tree strong and steady in its place. When we ground ourselves, we become like the tree, still and steady, no matter how much the wind might swirl around us. It's a simple technique with big results. Let's try it.

For You to Do

Take 5 is a grounding exercise you can do anytime and anywhere to get your emotional balance back. No one will even know you're doing it! All it takes is tuning into your five senses for a few minutes.

Before you start, take five deep breaths in through your nose and out through your mouth. (Remember Amygdala Annie? This calms her a little, which makes the exercise more effective.)

5. Notice and name (in your head) five things you see around you right now. They can be things like a tree outside, a pencil on the table, a book on a shelf, a hairband on the floor, or a stripe on the desk in front of you. Anything you can see counts.

4. Touch four things around you, and notice how they feel. You might pay attention to the smooth surface of the chair you are sitting on, the texture of your hair, the softness of the fabric of your shirt, and the bumpy edges of a pencil in your hand. Anything you can touch will work; just make sure you notice the feeling of the touch.

3. Listen to three things around you. If you tune your attention to sounds, you might notice the *whrrrr* of an air conditioner, the scratching sound of a pencil on paper, the tapping of keys on a keyboard. Listen for three separate sounds.

2. Smell two things around you. You might notice the scent of soap from when you washed your hands. You might smell the metal scent of your water bottle. You can do this subtly without drawing attention to yourself.

1. Taste one thing around you. This is most likely a taste already in your mouth. Focus on the taste in your mouth. Do you notice toothpaste from when you brushed your teeth in the morning?

When your head gets too overwhelmed, just use your senses and Take 5 to feel steady, calm, and back in control.

Henry couldn't be outside because his parents weren't home after school, and he had to stay inside until they got there. But Henry could go outside in his imagination. I'm outside in my backyard, *he thought to himself, closing his eyes.* There's a huge tree. I don't know what kind it is, but the bark is brown and the leaves are as big as fans, and when I lean against it, the trunk feels really strong and solid. I like to sit under this tree and lean against the trunk. It feels comfortable, and it feels safe. Everything seems a little more peaceful when I'm here under the tree. The ground feels nice and cool, the tree trunk I lean against is firm, the leaves from the tree make it shady underneath, and I like to listen to the bird sounds and sometimes even a cricket.

For You to Know

More and more research is showing that time outside in nature helps people feel better and recharge more easily. Some people find that their heart rate goes down and their breathing gets slower and deeper after time in nature. It's almost like nature can be an automatic reset for our stress levels. When we have less stress, we have more room for grit.

Scientists are learning that being outside in nature makes people feel more calm. Within twenty minutes of being in a green space (a park or forest, for example), people feel less stressed and happier. Human beings seem to be wired to feel better when they take time away from electronics and go outside in the fresh air. There's even research showing that people act nicer when they're outside more!

In Japan, there's a whole movement called Forest Bathing. No, you don't take a bath in the forest! You go into the woods, and you "bathe" in the beautiful trees, the leaves, the grass, the sounds, and the smells—the whole thing. You soak it all in. It's like a nature bath for your senses.

For You to Do

Some of us live in the country, where it's easy to find time in nature. Some of us live in the city, where soaking up nature is more of a challenge, but even in the city there are parks, grassy spots, and trees. In the square below, map out the areas close to you where you might go for a nature recharge. Include your favorite tree, a shady spot with a bench, or a grassy hill where you love to read.

Maybe that tree has a swing or a treehouse that's perfect for recharging. Maybe your bench is next to a garden with flowers and birds and squirrels you love to smell and hear and watch. Draw all of those things on your map if they help you recharge!

The Grit Workbook for Kids

More to Do

Do you look forward to vacation? Where is your favorite place to go? The mountains? A lake? Camping? The beach? While vacations are a great chance to recharge, they don't happen often. What if you could take a vacation any time you wanted to? We have an exercise that we call the three-minute vacation, and all you have to do is use your mind! Ready?

It can be helpful to have someone read this to you the first couple of times, but it's okay if there's no one around. Just open your eyes to read the text as needed, and then take a minute to refocus on the images after you've read. Or, you can read it yourself, record your voice, and then play it back. This is just for the first few times you practice it. Once you've taken your three-minute vacation a few times, it becomes easy to go there without any help.

Close your eyes and take three slow and deep breaths in through your nose and out through your mouth. As you breathe, notice that your muscles are relaxing, and your body is starting to feel heavy and calm. Inside your head, say to yourself, "I am calm. I am relaxed." Repeat this two or three times.

Now imagine you are walking down a path to a gate. There is a lovely wall around the gate. It is a strong and safe wall, and you can open the gate just by pressing your palm against the lock. Feel the cool metal as you open the gate.

Once you step inside the gate, you are in your favorite vacation spot in the whole world. You shut the gate behind you, and you notice all the beautiful things that make up your favorite vacation spot. Use your senses to notice and describe these things to yourself.

What do you see? Look from the sky to the ground, and everywhere in between. What are the images you see in your favorite vacation spot? Are there trees, grass, and butterflies? Sand, ocean waves, and shells littering the ground? Is there a lake with boats sailing on the surface, white puffy clouds, and birds hanging out in trees?

What is the temperature like? Is there a cool wind, a warm breeze? Is the air dry or humid? What are you wearing on your three-minute vacation? You, of course, are dressed perfectly for the environment.

Do you notice any smells? Is there a salty smell from ocean water? A fresh scent from pine trees? The smell of food cooking?

Reach down and touch the ground beneath you. Is it rocky and dry, soft and grassy? Is it light, warm, and sandy?

Are there any sounds? Water rushing, kids playing, seagulls chattering?

Who is there with you? It's your three-minute vacation so you get to bring whoever you want. Maybe your family is surrounding you with big smiles and laughter. Maybe it's you and your friends playing together outdoors, maybe you're walking with your dog or riding a horse.

Take a few minutes to really enjoy your surroundings. Quietly walk around and be present in this three-minute vacation. Notice as many details as you can, and let yourself feel the good feelings that come with this vacation.

When you're ready, go back to the gate you used to enter your three-minute vacation, and close it behind you as you leave. Now that you've been here, you can come back in your mind any time you want. This three-minute vacation is always available to you.

Do you feel more relaxed? Hopefully the exercise helped you feel calm and shrink any stress that may be bothering you. Sometimes we are stuck in a situation where we can't leave our seat or go outside to sit under a tree, but we can go to this spot in our mind. This can be a vacation away from stress or a vacation just to recharge. The best part about it is that you don't need plane tickets, parents, or anything else. Once we get used to visualizing (that's a fancy word for imagining) safe, calm places, we can bring up those images and thoughts whenever we want.

Keep It Going!

Your next step is to take the skills you've learned and use them in your real life. Let's review them:

Grit List

1. Look for grit.

2. Calm your brain down if it overreacts.

3. Recognize that your brain can change.

4. Name feelings to tame feelings.

5. Catch your thoughts to change your thoughts.

6. Use self-talk.

7. Use mantras that motivate.

8. Recognize the 3 Ps in action.

9. Change through growth thinking.

10. Choose to be grateful.

11. Check your perspective.

12. Try to see things the way the other person does.

13. Figure out what the real problem is.

14. Meet your needs for sleep, exercise, and eating.

15. Take time for yourself.

16. Ground and strengthen yourself through mindfulness.

The more you use the skills, the bigger your grit will grow. You can download a copy of this list at http://www.newharbinger.com/45984 and hang it on the door of your closet, the mirror in your bathroom, or anywhere else you can see it to remind you of all your grit-growing strategies.

Congratulations! You have worked hard to build your grit skills. At http://www.newharbinger.com/45984, you can download a copy of this certificate to celebrate your efforts. This workbook was the first step toward a lifelong practice of grit building!

CERTIFICATE
— OF GRIT —

AWARDED TO:

_____

AWARDED BY:

Elisa Nebolsine, LCSW

AUTHOR, THE GRIT WORKBOOK FOR KIDS

_____

CONGRATULATIONS ON BUILDING YOUR GRIT!

KEEP UP THE GRITTY WORK.

GRITTY KID!

Acknowledgments

I am deeply indebted to Jane Annunziata, who originally came up with the idea of a resilience workbook for kids. This workbook reflects the many hours Jane and I spent brainstorming and writing ideas for a "bounce back" guide
for kids. Jane's influence is sprinkled throughout this book, and her wisdom and mentorship were and are a bright light in my work.

The illustrations in this book were drawn by the talented Ali Hamdani. In addition to being a skilled artist, Ali is a patient and thoughtful collaborator. Polina Zimina drew the bold forms, and I am grateful for her work and beautiful drawings. Polina made grit forms bright and beautiful. Several of the online forms were sketched by Stefani Setiawan, and Stefani is a true professional and talented artist.

Elisa Nebolsine, LCSW, is owner and clinician at CBT for Kids, a private practice in Falls Church, VA. She is also adjunct faculty at the Beck Institute for Cognitive Behavior Therapy, adjunct faculty at Catholic University, and diplomate of the Academy of Cognitive Therapy. She has presented locally and nationally on the topic of cognitive behavioral therapy (CBT) and children, and is a consultant for schools, agencies, and other organizations on the implementation and use of CBT with children.

Foreword writer **Judith S. Beck, PhD**, is director of the Beck Institute for Cognitive Behavior Therapy and past president of the Academy of Cognitive Therapy. Daughter of influential founder of cognitive therapy, Aaron T. Beck, Beck is author of *The Beck Diet Solution*.

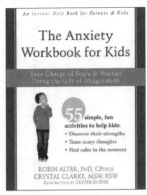

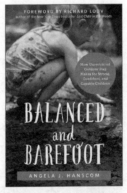
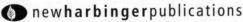

Register your **new harbinger** titles for additional benefits!

When you register your **new harbinger** title—purchased in any format, from any source—you get access to benefits like the following:

- Downloadable accessories like printable worksheets and extra content

- Instructional videos and audio files

- Information about updates, corrections, and new editions

Not every title has accessories, but we're adding new material all the time.

Access free accessories in 3 easy steps:

1. Sign in at NewHarbinger.com (or **register** to create an account).

2. Click on **register a book**. Search for your title and click the **register** button when it appears.

3. Click on the **book cover or title** to go to its details page. Click on **accessories** to view and access files.

That's all there is to it!

If you need help, visit:

NewHarbinger.com/accessories

new harbinger
CELEBRATING
40 YEARS